Tell Me Why

WHY?

I Get the Hiccups

Nancy Robinson Masters

Published in the United States of America by Cherry Lake Publishing
Ann Arbor, Michigan
www.cherrylakepublishing.com

Content Adviser: Charisse Gencyuz, M.D., Clinical Instructor, Department of Internal Medicine,
University of Michigan
Reading Adviser: Marla Conn, ReadAbility, Inc

Photo Credits: © Cherry-Merry/Shutterstock Images, cover, 1; © Mr.Nikon/Shutterstock Images, cover, 1;
© Pornthep Khetrum/Shutterstock Images, cover, 1; © Elena P./Shutterstock Images, 5; © udaix/Shutterstock
Images, 7; © Eraxion/CanStock Photo, 9; © maxim ibragimov/Shutterstock Images, 11; © Chris from Paris/
Shutterstock Images, 13; © Efired/Shutterstock Images, 15; © wavebreakmedia/Shutterstock Images, 17;
© Antonio Guillem/Shutterstock Images, 19; © racorn/Shutterstock Images, 21

Library of Congress Cataloging-in-Publication Data

Masters, Nancy Robinson, author.
 I get the hiccups / Nancy Robinson Masters.
    pages cm.—(Tell me why)
 Summary: "Young children are naturally curious about themselves. I Get the Hiccups offers answers to
their most compelling questions about hiccups and how to stop them. Age-appropriate explanations and
appealing photos encourage readers to continue their quest for knowledge. Additional text features and search
tools, including a glossary and an index, help students locate information and learn new words:—Provided by
publisher.
 Audience: Age 6–10.
 Audience: Grades K to 3.
 Includes bibliographical references and index.
 ISBN 978-1-63362-611-9 (hardcover)—ISBN 978-1-63362-701-7 (pbk.)—ISBN 978-1-63362-791-8 (pdf)
—ISBN 978-1-63362-881-6 (ebook)
 1. Hiccups—Juvenile literature. I. Title. II. Series: Tell me why (Cherry Lake Publishing)

QP372.M37 2016
612.2—dc23

                        2015005651

Cherry Lake Publishing would like to acknowledge the work of the Partnership for 21st Century Skills.
Please visit *www.p21.org* for more information.

Printed in the United States of America
Corporate Graphics

Table of Contents

Hic! Hic!

Caleb hurried to the principal's office. It was his turn to read the announcements to the entire school.

Suddenly, funny sounds came out of his mouth.

Hic! Hic! He had hiccups!

Hiccups can happen when you are nervous or excited.

What Is a Hiccup?

A hiccup is a sudden **spasm** of the **diaphragm** muscle. The diaphragm muscle is a large, thin sheet of stretchy tissue. It separates your lungs and heart from your stomach. A diaphragm muscle spasm causes the **vocal cords** in your throat to slam shut. This makes the "hic" sound that comes out of your mouth. It takes less than a second for this to happen.

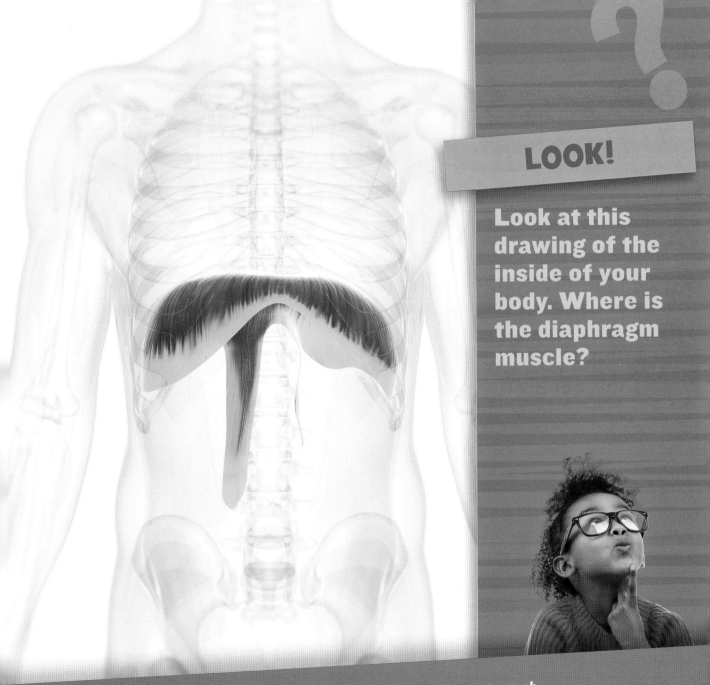

Look at this drawing of the inside of your body. Where is the diaphragm muscle?

The diaphragm separates your heart and lungs from your stomach.

The diaphragm also moves during normal breathing, but more steadily. When you inhale, or breathe in, it moves downward. This gives your lungs room to expand. When you exhale, or breathe out, it moves upward again as the air leaves your lungs.

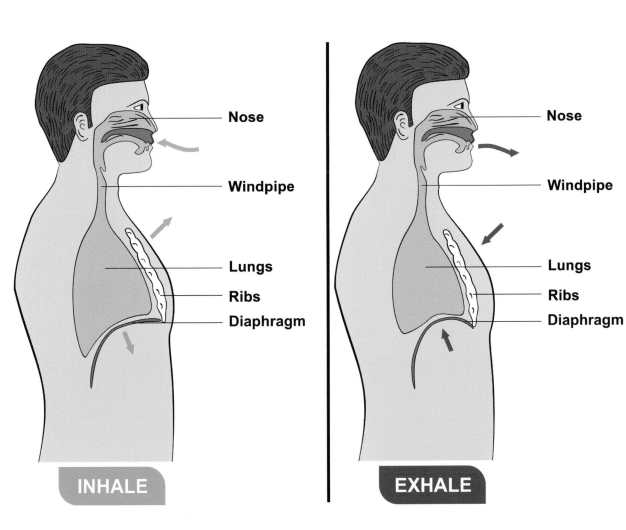

Nose

Windpipe

Lungs

Ribs

Diaphragm

INHALE

Nose

Windpipe

Lungs

Ribs

Diaphragm

EXHALE

Your diaphragm moves each time you breathe in or out.

What Causes Hiccups?

The diaphragm muscle is part of your **respiratory system**. The respiratory system is made up of **organs** you use to breathe. The **phrenic nerve** controls the diaphragm muscle. This nerve goes from your brain to your stomach. It is like a long electrical cord. It signals the diaphragm to help move air into and out of your lungs.

ASK QUESTIONS!

Visit the school nurse. Ask him or her to help you find information on how to avoid hiccups.

Covering your mouth when you hiccup is the polite thing to do.

Irritants can cause the phrenic nerve to send faulty signals to the diaphragm. These faulty signals result in spasms. The most common irritant is eating too much. Eating too fast is another. Swallowing air is a major irritant! Even feeling excited or scared can cause the diaphragm to spasm. When this happens, you may hiccup once or several times in a row.

Swallowing too much or eating too fast can cause hiccups.

How Do You Cure Hiccups?

Hiccups happen to almost everyone. Scientists believe boys have hiccups more often than girls. Some animals also hiccup.

Caleb knew his hiccups would stop in a few minutes. But this morning, he could not wait. He held his breath and slowly counted to 10. This **home remedy** to cure hiccups usually worked.

Eating a spoonful of peanut butter is one home remedy for hiccups.

There are other home remedies people use to stop hiccups. Quickly drinking three gulps of water is one. Biting on a lemon is another. Blowing into a paper sack is a popular remedy. So is eating a spoonful of sugar. Others believe that scaring someone will cure that person of the hiccups!

Scientists have studied hiccups for thousands of years. They still do not know why these home remedies cure hiccups. Or why they don't.

MAKE A GUESS!

What do you think is the best way to stop hiccups? Which one would you choose to do?

Making someone laugh by tickling them may stop their hiccups. It resets their diaphragm, and they can breathe again.

Caleb's hiccups were not a serious health problem. **Persistent hiccups** are another story. Persistent hiccups last for more than a day. They may last for years! These non-stop hiccups interrupt breathing and sleeping. They can keep people from having fun with their friends. Very few people have persistent hiccups. Those who do should go to the doctor for a checkup. They will need medical help to stop hiccupping.

Hold your breath and count to 10! This is the most popular cure for hiccups.

Caleb was glad his hiccups lasted only a few seconds. He read the morning announcements without a hic!

Later, Caleb found out that March 16 is National Hiccup Day. He will be sure to add that fact to the school announcements for that day! No one knows what year National Hiccup Day started, but people will be hiccuping for many more years to come.

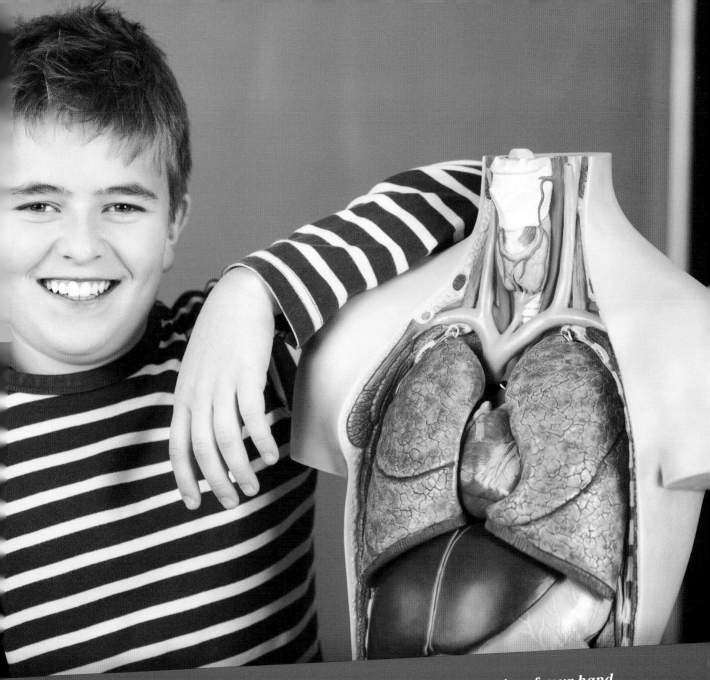

Your lungs are above your diaphragm. Each lung is about the size of your hand.

Think About It!

Charles Osborne hiccuped a world record 430 million times without stopping. How difficult would it be to live with persistent hiccups?

Think about having fun with a friend. Did you ever laugh so much you both got the hiccups? Why do you think this happened?

Why aren't chicken hiccups as loud as horse hiccups? Think about the size of each animal's diaphragm. Go online with an adult or visit a veterinarian to find out.

Glossary

diaphragm (DYE-uh-fram) the wall of muscle in your lower chest that draws air into and pushes air out of your lungs

home remedy (HOME REM-ih-dee) a natural way of curing a health problem without going to a doctor

irritants (IR-ih-tunts) things that cause soreness, sensitivity, or other discomfort to the body

organs (OR-guhnz) body parts that do special jobs

persistent hiccups (pur-SIST-unt HIK-uhps) hiccups that last more than a day

phrenic nerve (FREH-nik NURV) one of the threads that sends messages between your brain and body, in this case the one that controls the diaphragm muscle

respiratory system (RES-pur-uh-tor-ee SIS-tuhm) the group of organs used for breathing

spasm (SPAZ-uhm) a sudden tightening of a muscle that cannot be controlled

vocal cords (VOH-kuhl KORDZ) tissues in the throat that make sounds when air passes over them

Find Out More

Book:

Allyn, Daisy. *What Happens When I Hiccup?* Milwaukee: Gareth Stevens Publishing, 2014.

Web Sites:

KidsHealth: Lungs
http://kidshealth.org/kid/closet/movies/RSmovie.html?tracking=59983_C
Watch the diaphragm muscle in action.

Women's and Children's Health Network—Kids' Health: Hiccups and How to Get Rid of Them!
www.cyh.com/HealthTopics/HealthTopicDetailsKids.aspx?p=335&np=152&id=2412
Read more about hiccups and cures.

Index

About the Author

Nancy Robinson Masters is the author of more than 50 books. She and her husband, Bill, are airplane pilots. They live in the Elmdale community near Abilene, Texas. Nancy sometimes has hiccups when she is writing or flying.